Find Your Future in
Engineering

Diane Lindsey Reeves

Created and produced by
Bright Futures Press, Cary, North Carolina
www.brightfuturespress.com

Published by
Cherry Lake Publishing, Ann Arbor, Michigan
www.cherrylakepublishing.com

Photo Credits: cover, Shutterstock/Chekunov Aleksandr; cover, Shutterstock/Casper1774 Studios; cover, Shutterstock/Raimundas; cover, Shutterstock/bogdanhoda; cover, Shutterstock/yuyangc; page 4 (top), Shutterstock/TUMBARTSEV; page 4 (left), Shutterstock/royyimzy; page 6 (top), Shutterstock/ bogdanhoda; page 6 (left), Shutterstock/cigdem; page 7, Shutterstock/lvcadp; page 8, Shutterstock/ Andrey Yurlov; page 9 (top), Shutterstock/Raimundas; page 9 (left), Shutterstock/science photo; page 10, Shutterstock/baldyrgan; page 11, Shutterstock/www.BillionPhotos.com; page 12 (top), Shutterstock/stock photo mania; page 12 (left), Shutterstock/Luxrenedering; page 13, Shutterstock/TRONIN ANDREI; page 14, Shutterstock/Radoslaw Lecyk; page 15 (top), Shutterstock/Raimundas; page 15 (left), Shutterstock/ Everett Collection; page 16, Shutterstock/Julien Tromeur; page 17, Shutterstock/Sergey Nivens; page 18 (top), Shutterstock/Casper1774 Studio; page 18 (left), Shutterstock/Green Leaf; page 19, Shutterstock/ olga1818; page 20, Shutterstock/bokan; page 21 (top), Shutterstock/Alexlukin; 21 (left), Shutterstock/ grafvision; page 22, Shutterstock/Sudowoodo; page 23, Shutterstock/supergenijalac; page 24 (top), Shutterstock/Chekunov Aleksandr; page 24 (left), Shutterstock/Michael D Brown; page 25, Shutterstock/ AXpop; page 26, Shutterstock/Alexander Kirch; page 27 (top), Shutterstock/Praphan Jampala; page 27 (left), Shutterstock/Tatiana Popova; page 28, Shutterstock/Gianluca D. Muscelli; page 29, Shutterstock/ Caracarafoto.

Library of Congress Cataloging-in-Publication Data

Names: Reeves, Diane Lindsey, 1959- author.
Title: Find your future in engineering / by Diane Lindsey Reeves.
Description: Ann Arbor, Michigan : Cherry Lake Publishing, [2016] | Series:
  Find your future in STEAM | Audience: Grades 4 to 6. | Includes index.
Identifiers: LCCN 2016006908| ISBN 9781634719001 (hardcover) | ISBN
  9781634719469 (pbk.) | ISBN 9781634719230 (pdf) | ISBN 9781634719698
  (ebook)
Subjects: LCSH: Engineering--Vocational guidance--Juvenile literature.
Classification: LCC TA157 .R385 2016 | DDC 620.0023--dc23
LC record available at https://lccn.loc.gov/2016006908

Printed in the United States of America.

Table of Contents

Find Your Future in Engineering

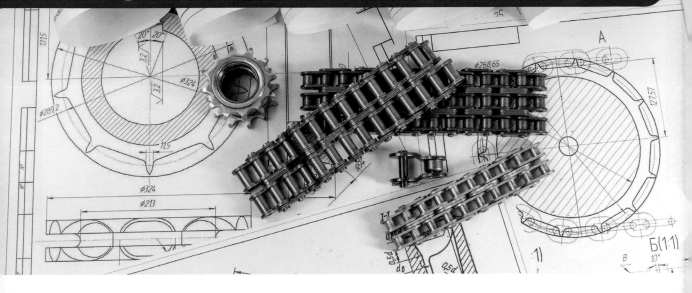

Find your future in engineering

How do **engineers** make the world a better place? Thanks to engineers, we have highways and bridges, skyscrapers, and schools. We have power systems, transportation systems, and clean water systems. Engineers bring us machines of all kinds. Robots, rocket ships, and even roller coasters get their start in the minds and on the computers of engineers. Engineers design and build the world we live, play, and work in.

Hooray for engineers!

Even though they work in many different fields, all engineers have two things in common. They like science and math. They also studied hard and got good grades in these subjects when they were in elementary school, middle school, and high school. They went on to graduate with college degrees. Once engineers start working, they use math and science every day in their jobs.

This book (and the other titles in the *Find Your Future* series) is especially for kids who like math, science, and machines! It will show you some of the amazing careers you can have when you get really good in these subjects. Read this book to find out how people use engineering to change the world and imagine how engineering can change your future. Browse through the career ideas featured in the following pages and ...

Surf the 'Net!

Type the words in **bold** in the Surf the 'Net sections into your favorite Internet search engine (like Google, Bing, or Yahoo) to find more information about the subject. Be sure to have permission and SUPERVISION from a trusted adult (like a teacher or parent) when using the Internet.

Explore Some More!

In this book you'll find ideas you can use to explore cool resources in websites, in the news, and in fun, online games. Here's your chance to goof around and learn some more.

Ask Big Questions!

Curiosity opens the door to learning (and fun!). Ponder the questions posed here. Each question comes with an activity you can do. Use them to share your answers through posters, games, presentations, or even a good discussion where you consider both sides of an idea.

**Go online to download free activity sheets at
www.cherrylakepublishing.com/activities.**

Aerospace Engineer

Surf the 'Net!

Take off by exploring the **history of flight**.

Can you imagine what it must have been like to be Wilbur and Orville Wright on December 17, 1903? For years, the brothers had been working to design a machine that let people fly like birds.

Other people tried to do this. But all had failed in one way or another. People said it was impossible for humans to fly. Lots of people thought it was crazy to even try. After all, if humans were meant to fly, we would have been born with wings. Right?

But on that fateful day in Kitty Hawk, North Carolina, the Wright brothers succeeded! Wilbur took off and soared through the sky 892 feet (272 meters) above the ground. He flew for 59 seconds before safely landing the plane. He was the first person in history to fly a power-driven, heavier-than-air airplane.

But Wilbur certainly wasn't the last. The machine they called "Flyer" opened the door to all the high-flying wonders we know today. The Wright brothers are considered the fathers of modern aviation. They still inspire the **aerospace engineers** who continue to find new ways to fly.

Aerospace engineers work with anything that flies in air or in space. Some aerospace engineers design and build airplanes, jets, helicopters, and rockets. Others design satellites and national defense systems. During the past century, aerospace engineers have achieved remarkable results in both areas.

Just getting an airplane off the ground was a big deal a hundred years ago. Now you

Ask Big Questions!

Drones are unmanned aircraft, or ships guided by remote control or onboard computers. Drones are gaining in popularity, and many people have high hopes for using drones in interesting ways. **What would the world be like if drones could deliver pizza?** Draw a picture of how this might look in your neighborhood.

Explore Some More!

Engineer different types of paper airplanes found at **www.foldnfly.com**.

can board a plane in Los Angeles and fly all the way across the country to New York City in just a few hours. People fly across oceans and around the world every day. Visit any airport and you will see how flight has progressed since 1903. It is amazing!

The 21st century is also bringing exciting new opportunities for aerospace engineers working with spacecraft. Space stations, robotic probes, manned missions to other planets, and colonies on the moon offer real possibilities for future aerospace engineers.

It makes you wonder what Wilbur and Orville would think of all this progress. After all, they were just two brothers who wanted to fly like a bird.

Humans can now fly, thanks to the wonders of scientific ingenuity.

Chemical Engineer

Surf the 'Net!

Get acquainted with **chemical engineers in action** and find out more about exciting innovations in this field.

Did you realize that your body is made up of a chemical soup? It's true. Six elements make up almost 99 percent of the mass of your body. Those elements are **oxygen**, **carbon**, **hydrogen**, **nitrogen**, **calcium**, and **phosphorus**.

Humans aren't alone in being made of chemicals. According to the American Chemical Society, there are more than 106 million unique organic and inorganic chemical substances on record. And the list

9

of new chemical substances grows bigger every minute! **Chemical engineers** create food products, medicines, energy, and electronics using these chemicals.

Many chemical engineers are working hard to help the environment. Many of the chemicals currently used in manufacturing and other industries create air or water **pollution**. Safer chemicals will help keep our air and waterways clean and healthy.

Chemical engineers are also busy developing new energy solutions using solar power, wind, and other renewable fuel sources. Of course, chemical engineers still work with traditional fuel sources, like coal.

Chemical engineers and other scientists are developing new ways to deliver lifesaving medicines. Their discoveries help people live longer and healthier lives. They also help doctors diagnose and treat diseases by using a patient's DNA to personalize medicine in new ways.

One big medical accomplishment is in the area of artificial knees and hips. Chemical

Ask Big Questions!

What chemicals are in the products you use every day? Grab a notebook and start a scavenger hunt through your house. Make a list of the products you find that are made up of chemicals. Check your food pantry, the garage, the bathroom medicine cabinet, and more. Be prepared to make a very long list!

engineers now use a unique combination of materials to make artificial joints that last longer and are more comfortable and flexible than those used in the past. This is great news for anyone who needs to have worn out joints replaced.

Food is another big area where chemical engineers work to find better ways to feed the world. Just look at the weird names of some of the ingredients listed on food labels and it is clear that chemical engineers have had a hand in the recipes.

Chemical engineers have already accomplished amazing things. Stay tuned for more exciting developments in this field!

Explore Some More!

Enjoy some chemistry adventures at **www. acs.org/content/ acs/en/education/ whatischemistry/ adventures-in- chemistry.html**.

Chemical engineers often work in laboratories.

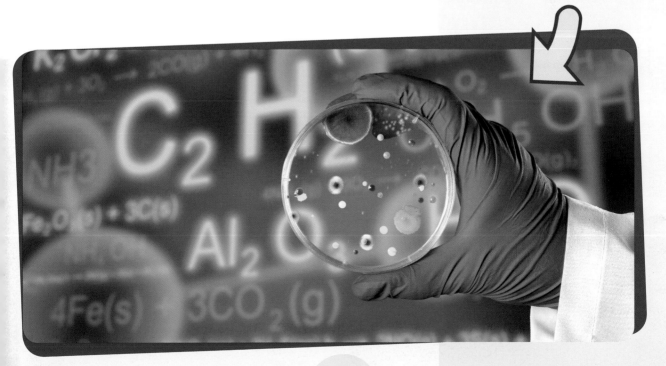

Civil Engineer

What do the Golden Gate Bridge, Hoover Dam, and the Grand Canyon Skywalk have in common? They are all examples of awesome civil engineering!

Civil engineers design and maintain the public places we share. This includes roads, bridges, and water and energy systems. It also includes ports, railways, airports, and subway systems. When it comes to projects civil engineers work on, you need to think big!

Surf the 'Net!

Prepare to be impressed when you see the **Seven Wonders of the World**. Try to imagine what it must have been like to build these structures.

Safety comes first when planning structures for people. Highways must be built to handle the thousands and thousands of cars and trucks that travel on them each day. Skyscrapers must be built to stand in all kinds of weather, including earthquakes. Transportation centers, like airports, train stations, and subways, must be designed to get people and vehicles moving in lots of different directions at the same time. No small feat!

You'd have to travel all the way to Egypt and go back in time thousands of years to see some of the first known civil engineers in action. Long before the days of big trucks, cranes, and fancy tools, Egyptians built amazing pyramid-shaped tombs that were over 480 feet (146 meters) tall! One of these pyramids still stands today in Giza. It is celebrated as one of the **Seven Wonders of the World**.

Not all the work that civil engineers do makes history like the pyramids and the Great Wall of China. But when they get it right, the work will last for a very

Ask Big Questions!

What does it take to engineer a bridge that works? See what you can find out about how to build a structurally strong bridge. Then get out your Legos®, popsicle® sticks, or straws, and use them to build a bridge that won't fall down.

Explore Some More!

Visit the American Society of Civil Engineers' website for kids at **www.asceville. org** to explore what civil engineers do.

long time. Civil engineers make life better and safer for people around the world.

America's 31st president and a former engineer himself, Herbert Hoover, once said about engineering, "It is a great profession. There is the fascination of watching a figment of the imagination emerge through the aid of science to a plan on paper. Then it moves to realization in stone or metal or energy. Then it brings jobs and homes to men (and women). Then it elevates the standards of living and adds to the comforts of life. That is the engineer's high privilege."

Well said, President Hoover, well said!

Awesome structures like these get their start in the minds of civil engineers.

Computer Engineer

Surf the 'Net!

Before you can be part of where computers are going, you need to understand where they have been. Find out more by searching for history of computers for kids.

Once upon a time, the first general purpose computer was as big as a room. It weighed 30 tons, and it used punch cards to process data. Its official name was Electronic Numerical Integrator and Computer (ENIAC), but people called it the "giant brain." This was back in 1946.

Fast-forward several decades. Today's smartphones have more computer power than NASA did in 1969, when it sent astronauts to the moon! Now that's progress! And kind of scary to think that men were wandering around the moon without the technologies we take for granted today.

Computer engineers continue to work to make computers, smartphones, and other digital devices faster, smaller, cheaper, and smarter. They design electronic systems for automobiles, kitchen appliances, robots, and pretty much anything you can imagine that uses technology.

Some work on the systems side, developing software that solves problems, helps people communicate, and entertains. Other computer engineers work on the hardware side. They design the devices that people use for business, communication, and just for fun.

When you get right down to it, computer engineers are the super heroes of technology. They come up with the next big ideas in smart devices and other electronic gizmos that we love to use for work and play. When they tackle a problem, the

Ask Big Questions!

We have smartphones, smart watches, and super sleek laptops. **What kind of technology do you suppose people will be using in the future?** Draw a picture of your ideas and use words to describe them.

solution is quite often new state-of-the-art (translated: totally cool!) products.

So far, computer power has doubled every 18 to 24 months. It's something called **Moore's Law**. If computer engineers keep up this pace, then computers 100 years from now would be 1,125,899,906,842,624 times more powerful than they are today. Whoa!

Yours is the first digital generation. Your parents and grandparents didn't always have access to today's cell phones and tablets. Someday the technologies we now think of as awesome will be obsolete and seem as old-fashioned as an 8-track tape deck. (You'll have to ask your grandparents what that was!)

Explore Some More!

Program your own interactive stories, games, and animations in an online community at scratch.mit.edu.

Computer engineers design the inside systems and the outside components of digital devices.

Environmental Engineer

Surf the 'Net!

Find out how you can be more earth-friendly by following the three Rs: **reduce, recycle, reuse**.

Environmental engineers are problem solvers. Some work on fixing problems that have already happened. Others work on solving problems before they happen. All environmental engineers work to make sure that the 7 billion people who share our planet have clean air and water. They also work to make sure that people have safe places to live, work, and play.

One of the big problems now being tackled is pollution. Most of the world depends on fossil fuels for energy, like oil, coal, and natural gas. These natural resources are used to fuel cars and airplanes, power electrical plants, and to heat homes and businesses.

Then there are the chemicals used in homes, farms, and businesses. All these things are very useful. But they also cause air and water pollution.

Environmental engineers help clean up messes made by pollution. They design systems, processes, and equipment to restore air, soil, and water quality. For instance, environmental engineers might design a wastewater system that uses microbes or fungi to clean contaminated water at a factory.

Other environmental engineers work just as hard to prevent pollution from happening. They work to make renewable energy sources, like solar and wind power, available to more people. They work to find alternative fuels from corn, algae, and other creative sources. It's all about going "**green**" and finding earth-friendly solutions.

Ask Big Questions!

The average American throws away 4.5 pounds of trash every day. **What can you do at home and school to reduce and recycle trash?** Come up with at least three terrific ideas and make a poster to share your tips.

Explore Some More!

Go online to visit the Environmental Protection Agency's Recycle City game at www3.epa.gov/recyclecity.

Human waste is another problem that keeps environmental engineers looking for better solutions. We've come a long way since the days when devastating epidemics like Bubonic plague, cholera, and typhoid fever were caused by poor waste management. But, poop still happens. There are 2.5 billion people who live in places without safe waste management systems.

All environmental engineers share a common goal: to leave the earth in better shape than they found it. That way, future generations (like yours!) can enjoy happy and healthy lives on the planet we call home.

Finding better ways to manage landfills is what some environmental engineers do.

Manufacturing Engineer

Surf the 'Net!

Search for **how stuff gets made** to learn how some of your favorite products are manufactured.

What do baseballs, automobiles, and store-bought chocolate chip cookies have in common? Besides the fact that they are all round, they are all manufactured in **factories**! Not at the same factory, of course, but still...

Manufacturing engineers are involved in figuring out the best ways to produce products for mass consumption. The goal is always to make high-quality products as quickly and inexpensively as possible.

In other words, better, cheaper, faster is the name of the manufacturing game—no matter what product you are producing.

Henry Ford didn't invent the automobile, as some people think. In 1913, he invented a better way to make cars. Ford's **assembly line** involved simply moving the car to the workers. The change was brilliant. It reduced the time it took to make a car from 12 hours to about 90 minutes. It also reduced the price of a Model T from $850 to less than $300. People no longer had to be rich to buy a car. Goodbye, horse and buggy. Hello, automobile!

So much has changed in manufacturing that Mr. Ford would not recognize a modern factory. But he would, no doubt, be impressed. Today, manufacturing engineers use high-tech machines, **3-D printing**, and even robots to **automate** production processes. Working in factories on assembly lines used to mean repeating the same task over and over again. Workers were trained to perform specific tasks.

Ask Big Questions!

How can you make a favorite product faster and better? Pick a product like brownies, bracelets, or baseball bats. Make a chart to show the steps you would take to make your product.

Today's manufacturing jobs require highly skilled workers. Even so, manufacturing sometimes gets a bum rap. Some people think of it as dirty work in dark sweatshops with long hours and low pay. They think of manufacturing jobs as boring, repetitious, and even dangerous. Modern manufacturing breaks this mold with many high-tech opportunities, using state-of-the-art equipment.

Experts say there will be a big demand for people to do manufacturing jobs when you grow up. Jobs on the horizon are high-tech with higher-than-average pay. It's a new world in manufacturing!

Explore Some More!

Discover why manufacturing is cool at **www. manufacturingiscool. com**.

Modern technology plus Henry Ford's assembly line equals great progress in manufacturing.

Mechanical Engineer

Surf the 'Net!

Search for **how machines work** to get the inside scoop on how amazing products do what they do.

Did you turn on a light today? Did you turn on a water faucet to wash your hands? Did you ride in a car, train, or airplane? Did you use a computer? Maybe, if you were lucky, you went for a stroll on a walking escalator at an airport, or you went for a whirl on a roller coaster.

All these **machines** and gadgets—and so many more—are possible because of **mechanical engineers**. Mechanical engineers design power-producing machines. Anything that you can turn on and off has likely been worked on by a mechanical engineer. If you are thinking that mechanical engineers must work in many different industries, you are correct.

Auto, aerospace, medical, manufacturing, construction, military, and electronics are just a few of the industries that benefit from the talents of mechanical engineers. They make toys and turbojet engines, refrigerators and rocket ships. If a product moves, mechanical engineers are involved in designing and producing it.

As in other engineering fields, computers have changed the way mechanical engineers do their jobs. Technology helps them answer questions about how and why something works. It lets them test all kinds of "what-if" situations. Using computers, they **simulate** and test how a machine is supposed to work.

New technologies, like 3-D printing, are making the profession even more exciting.

Ask Big Questions!

Pick a favorite machine. It might be a car, a drone, or even a hair dryer. **How has your favorite machine changed over time?** Make a chart with three columns. Use one column to show what this machine was like in the "past." In the second column, show what it is like now, in the "present." Use the third column to imagine what it might be like in the "future."

Explore Some More!

Ready to discover the world of mechanical engineering? Go online to **www.thinkmech.ca/kids**.

Need new golf balls? There's no need to go shopping when your personal 3-D printer can do the job!

Instead of printing out words on a sheet of paper, 3-D printing lets engineers 'print' out actual products. Mechanical engineers download a file, click the print button, and—presto—out comes a **prototype** of a complex product. Of course, the magic is in those files. Mechanical engineers must provide very technical instructions to get the results they want.

It is quite possible that 3-D printing could change manufacturing as much or more than Henry Ford's assembly line, by making the design process faster, and product-testing easier. Technologies like these help mechanical engineers design the future.

Robotics Engineer

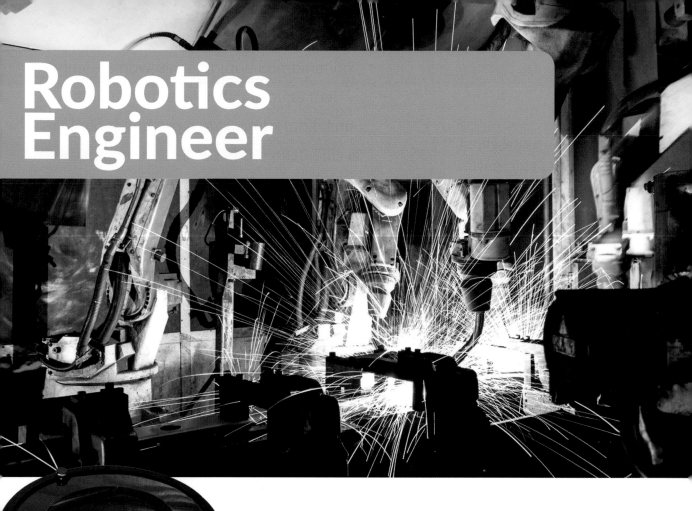

Surf the 'Net!

Look into the **history of robots for kids** to see what has already been achieved and get an idea of what is yet to come.

"Robot, clean my room!"

"Robot, do my homework!"

"Robot, eat my broccoli!"

Robots have come a long way. They can already do many chores. But there are still some things that robots can't do. Picking up smelly socks, studying for math tests, and eating veggies are still up to you!

Robots are machines that are programmed to automatically do specific tasks. They often perform humanlike actions. **Robotics engineers** design robots to go places people can't go, and to do things people don't want to do. Robots are especially useful in manufacturing where some tasks must be performed over and over *and over* again.

Big retailers use robots to help employees move products around in huge warehouses. The robots do the heavy lifting, and the humans are able to triple the amount of work they complete. Robots save lives on battlefields by taking apart land mines and bombs. They help farmers harvest crops. They even help doctors perform life-saving surgeries that are less painful for patients.

Robotic engineers are working on big ideas that could change our future. Imagine if someday teeny, tiny **nanorobots** could be swallowed and used to diagnose and treat serious illnesses. What if wearable robots could help blind people see and hearing-impaired people hear? It's quite likely that robots will soon be used to explore the ocean floor and outer space.

Ask Big Questions!

If you could invent a robot, what would you want it to do? Draw a picture and describe how your robot might improve life for people and make the world a better place.

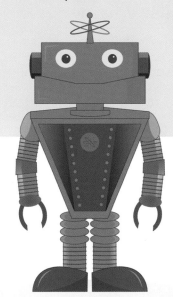

When it comes right down to it, robots are turning up in all kinds of places these days. Some robotic engineers are experimenting with self-driving cars. Others are working to develop mechanical butlers that deliver snacks to hotel guests. Researchers are even trying to design robots that can teach themselves to perform common tasks, like cooking dinner by watching YouTube videos.

There is no doubt that robots are here to stay. What no one knows for sure is how they will change our lives. Who knows, someone (maybe even you!) may invent a robot that can tackle the tasks that you dislike! Now about those veggies...

Explore Some More!

Build your own virtual robot online at www. wonderville.ca/asset/ robot-factory.

Robots are changing the way people work in many amazing ways.

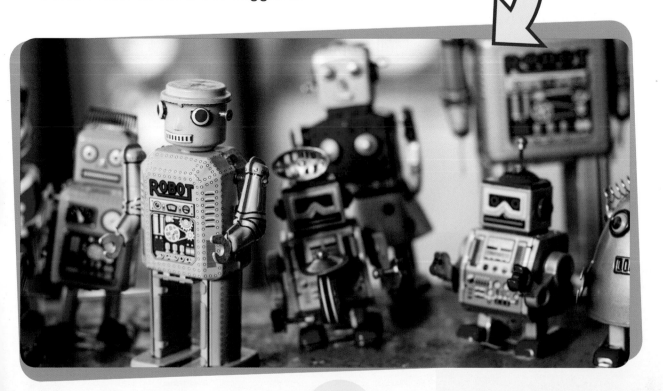

Find *Your* Future in Engineering

Let's review the amazing career ideas you've just discovered. Below are descriptions of some of the opportunities waiting for people who like engineering. Read them and see if you can match them with the correct job titles.

Instead of writing in this book, use a separate sheet of paper to write your answers and imagine your future! Even better, download a free activity sheet at wwwcherrylakepublishing.com/ activities.

A Aerospace engineer

B Chemical engineer

C Civil engineer

D Computer engineer

E Environmental engineer

F Manufacturing engineer

G Mechanical engineer

H Robotics engineer

1 Figure out the world's most efficient way to make millions of chocolate chip cookies

2 Design an environmentally-friendly school

3 Find new ways to preserve packaged food with healthy ingredients

4 Build the world's tallest skyscraper

5 Invent a wearable computer that is built into sneakers

6 Design the first flying car

7 Design a robot that helps doctors diagnose and treat diseases like cancer

8 Use 3-D printing to design a new jet engine

(Answer Key: 1-F; 2-E; 3-B; 4-C; 5-D; 6-A; 7-H; 8-G)

30

Glossary

3-D printing the process of making solid, three-dimensional objects from a digital file

aerospace engineer person who designs and develops aircraft and spacecraft

assembly line combination of machines, equipment, and workers in which products pass from operation to operation in a direct line until a product is assembled

automate to do something using machines instead of people

calcium mineral found mostly in the hard part of bones

carbon one of the basic chemical elements of any living thing

chemical engineer person who works in the chemical industry to convert basic raw materials into a variety of products

civil engineer person who designs and maintains roads, bridges, dams, and similar public structures

computer engineer person who designs computer software, hardware, networks, and systems

engineers people who are scientifically trained to design and build complicated products, machines, systems, or structures

environmental engineer person who works to improve and maintain the environment for the protection of human health and at-risk ecosystems

factories buildings or groups of buildings where products are manufactured

green earth-friendly processes and practices

hydrogen the simplest, lightest, and most abundant chemical element in the universe

machines equipment with moving parts that work when given power from electricity, gasoline, or another source of energy

manufacturing engineer person who researches, designs, and develops the systems, processes, machines, tools, and equipment used to manufacture products

mechanical engineer person who designs and produces machinery

Moore's Law prediction by Intel co-founder, Gordon Moore, that processor speeds, or overall processing power for computers, will double every two years

nanorobots machines made from individual atoms or molecules that are designed to perform a small and specific job

nitrogen chemical element found in four-fifths of the earth's atmosphere and in the tissues of living things

oxygen chemical element found in the air as a colorless, odorless, and tasteless gas that is necessary for life

phosphorous mineral that makes up one percent of a person's body weight

pollution unwanted, harmful substances or things that contaminate an environment

prototype the first version of an invention that tests an idea to see if it will work

robotics engineer person who designs, constructs, and operates robots

Seven Wonders of the World seven most spectacular, man-made structures of the ancient world

simulate to copy or imitate a process or procedure

Index

About the Author

Diane Lindsey Reeves is the author of lots of children's books including several original PEANUTS stories (published by Regnery Kids and Sourcebooks). She is especially curious about what people do and likes to write books that get kids thinking about all the cool things they can be when they grow up. Reeves lives in Cary, North Carolina and her favorite thing to do is play with her grandkids – Conrad, Evan, and Reid Clasen and Hollis Grace Palmer.